# FIVE LETTERS

# FIVE LETTERS

## MICHAEL PSEULLOS

Copyright 2025 by Dalcassian Press

All rights reserved. No part of this book may be reproduced in any manner whatsoever without written permission except in the case of brief quotations embodied in critical articles and reviews.
No part of this publication may be reproduced, distributed, or transmitted in any form or by any means, including photocopying, recording, or other electronic or mechanical methods, without the prior written permission of the publisher, except in the case of brief quotations embodied in critical reviews and certain other non-commercial uses permitted by copyright law. For permission request, write to Dalcassian Press at admin@thescriptoriumproject.com

Translator: Curtin, D.P. (1985-)
Translator: Hatzi, N.M. (1987-)

ISBN: 979-8-3482-5281-6(Paperback)
ISBN: 979-8-3482-5292-2 (eBook)
Library of Congress Control Number:

Printed by Ingram Content Group, 1 Ingram Blvd, La Vergne, Tennessee
First Printing 2024, Dalcassian Press, Wilmington, DE

This work is part of a series produced in association with the Scriptorium Project and its community of scholars and translators.
Please visit our website at: www.thescriptoriumproject.com

# Contents

1. To a Professor at the University    1
2. To my fellow student Romanos    5
3. To an Unnamed student    7
4. To the Metropolitan Vasileon Sinetus    9
5. To the monastic John Xiphilinos    11

# 1

# To a Professor at the University

It is best to remain silent, says the tragic poet Sophocles. But can one find the strength to remain silent in misfortunes, especially those as dreadful and tormenting as those that have befallen me? When one speaks of the most terrible things, one finds relief; therefore, I will tell you a little about how everything began. They held the wedding, and with its splendor, it overshadowed all other weddings. The bridal hall shone with beauty, hymns were sung, flutes played harmoniously, everything was full of joy, but nothing delighted me there; everything in the house weighed on me, and I prayed to God to free me from this marriage as soon as possible. The Lord looked upon me, heard my prayer, and shortly thereafter, I became free. Freed from the anxieties of marriage, considering that I had escaped from the storm and reached a quiet harbor, I offered a sacrifice of thanksgiving to God and longed to return to those pursuits we had agreed upon before, eager to enjoy learning from you. But some demon, envious and vengeful, unable to bear my happiness, forced me to think of something else, advised and convinced me to approach studies with scrutiny, to see only profits and losses, forgetting everything else. Listening to him—why did I do this!—I bid farewell to life in the capital and to the lessons of dear, beloved rhetoric, boarded a ship, and set my course toward the holy fathers. As I sailed to them, our Agros lay to our right, where we hoped to arrive. Now listen to what happened to us during the voyage. We boarded the ship early in the morning, for it was a great Sunday, celebrated by the fathers as a holiday. There were more than twelve of us travelers, plus three sailors. At first, the ship sailed close to the shore, and the coasts flashed by us; then we went out into the open sea, and suddenly a headwind blew. It was not very strong and did not trouble us at all. Soon, however, out of nowhere, a cloud appeared, the wind died down, and drops began to fall, first rare, then more frequent, until finally, a downpour poured down as if after someone's blow, so that we forgot about the direct path to the fathers and hurried to reach the harbor of the aforementioned Agros and bring the ship to the dock. When we finally managed to do this, albeit with difficulty, we disembarked and went to Agros. After a short stay there, we began to think about returning, wishing to see the smoke of our homeland, and we boarded the ship again and set sail. It was already daytime, and the sea, lightly covered with waves, looked calm, promising us nothing bad. After sailing more than two stadia, we again went out into the open sea, and this time it was not smooth and calm, as at the beginning of the journey, but fierce and terrifying; it roared from the winds like a boiling cauldron. The waves swept over our ship, and the abyss would have swallowed us if the helmsman had not thought to turn the ship back and, noticing a harbor on the shore, had not brought us to land, not as the Phaeacians did with Odysseus, not asleep, but awake and frightened. When we were brought to shore and stepped onto dear land, we walked for a while, but as soon as the sea winds calmed down, we bravely set sail again and encountered storms several more times before we arrived here. As for what happened afterward, there are no words to describe it. We were struck by a plague, a painful and tormenting illness, preventing us from drinking or eating. Because of it, although we were encouraged by people who had already suffered from it, we lay barely alive, thinking about

Hades. Do not refuse to visit me while I am so ill, but come quickly to bid farewell to me before I die.

# 2

# To my fellow student Romanos

I think you have not completely forgotten our friendship, my beloved lord, a friendship we promised to cherish back when we engaged in common pursuits, spending time together and learning the sciences together. If this is so, as I believe, in you still burns at least a small spark of the former friendship, if it has not entirely extinguished or dissipated, and time has not darkened it, nor has friendship that came afterward diminished it or entangled it in forgetfulness, then show it now, and I will believe you. To prove it, fulfill my request. This request is not too great and not impossible. I will now present it to you. Two diligent young men come to our classes in orthography. Naturally clever and hardworking, they have already managed to go through most of the exercises I once compiled, and they now insistently urge us to beg for them from others, lamenting that not everyone absorbs them. Not knowing what to offer them, I turn to you, my true friend, reasoning that this honor should be bestowed on no one else but your good soul. For you have a treasure trove of exercises, and to speak the truth, a hive where you, like a hardworking bee, have stored all the beautiful and useful things you have gathered from flowers; you have the very best and most difficult exercises. I think this honor is neither great nor burdensome; you would not act in a friendly manner if you rejected my request. See that no one from your descendants holds it against you.

# 3

# To an Unnamed student

In the art of words, my dearest, I imitate painters; I do not immediately write a finished verbal image, nor do I create a teaching or refutation from the first, as they say, letter. Instead, I first make a general sketch and, as if casting a light shadow, I insert embellishments in this way and introduce a likeness corresponding to the depicted face. I learned this not from painters but borrowed it from philosophy. Indeed, in it, what precedes the science itself is very important: introductory parts, general sketches of what will be discussed, as well as conclusions. Therefore, do not think that the dispute is over, that in what I have already written, all accusations against your letter have been presented. If Timarchus, who made an unlawful accusation of bribery in the public assembly, was driven away by the orator Aeschines with a long speech, how can I not unleash an even longer speech against you, who have not stained yourself but tried to harm speeches, dared to look philosophy in the eye, and thus audaciously opposed me, its secret guide? You have not only tried to destroy one philosophy; you have risen against rhetorical speeches, and the legal science, from which, like from an acropolis, you have collapsed upon us, has long been crushed by you. To whom among the three shall I first allow to speak about how you have criminally dealt with it? Do you want rhetoric to express this to you? Here it stands, not in a Gorgian manner, not in a Hippian manner, not audaciously like Paul, but in a Demosthenic manner, holding itself with dignity, like proper upbringing itself. If its voice is not entirely clear to you (for its language is purely Attic and far from ordinary speech in many ways), I will interpret for you what it pronounces silently and indistinctly for you.

# 4

# To the Metropolitan Vasileon Sinetus

Why, honest soul, did I receive partridges along with the letter? Could it not be done without partridges? Do the wings of partridges lighten the weight of the letter? The proverb seems true: "If carrying a goat is a torment, then throw me a bull as well"? Why do you slander Vasileon, dressing in such poverty? Do not grains bear fruit there? Do not goats graze? Are not the grasses juicy? Do not the mountains rise, and the wide valleys stretch? I am familiar with it; I have bathed there and swum in warm springs. And the then prelate even gifted me a black mare with shiny skin and soft covers, on which we recline and with which we cover ourselves. Or has everything changed around, and the vine has brought figs? Well, do not send me anything but letters; their harvests have not diminished in Vasileon, for it is upbringing that bears fruit here, not the plain, souls, not the mountains. For your sake, let the valleys be filled, and let the uneven paths become smooth; let the fruits ripen, and let pears be born on pines, as it is said in the bucolic, and, if you wish, taste them all yourself, one by one, without counting. And for me, my books and the fruits that grow on them are enough. If someone were to take them away, I would not lament. I would i

# 5

# To the monastic John Xiphilinos

No, I will not give up Plato, the holiest and wisest [father]! He is mine, oh earth and sun, – I will exclaim, like a tragic figure on the verbal stage. You disparage my long readings of dialogues, my admiration for his style, and my reverence for his proofs. But why do you not reproach the great fathers? For they too cast syllogisms to overthrow the heresies of Eunomius and Apollinaris. If you think that I heed his dogmas or rely on his laws, then you judge us wrongly, brother.

I have uncovered many wise books, pronounced many rhetorical words, and, I will not deceive, neither has Plato hidden from me, nor have I scorned Aristotelian wisdom. I am familiar with the traditions of the Chaldeans and Egyptians. Yes, I know them, your honest head! And should I even speak of the forbidden books? But compared to our God-bearing Scripture, pure and bright, truly true, I have deemed everything else a lie and deception. No, I will not give up Plato! I do not even know how I will endure the severity of your speech! Was it not I who once loved the divine cross, and now the spiritual yoke? Are you not too strict, I reproach you with your own words? You have not refuted a single one of his thoughts, while I have refuted almost all of them, if one does not think that they are all bad. His speeches on justice and the immortality of souls guided us when we began to reason about such matters. Of course, I did not take the pus from there, but loved the pure moisture and strained it from the dirt.

I might still endure your blows, but only a soul of adamant and insensible, believe me, can listen to you about Chrysippus, about my syllogisms, about non-existent lines and everything else. Why did you not continue your speech, why did you not say: "Beware, unheard tortures await you!"

Everything you have written has stunned me, and I pondered for a long time until I suspected one of two things: either you did not read my letter, or you wrote to some Eunomius, or to the students of Cleanthes and Zeno, who, having placed everything on syllogisms, see nothing outside of calculations and proofs. Plato also examined them, having risen to speculation, he saw what lies beyond reason, focusing [attention] on the One, and you blame him for everything, hater of Plato and hater of words, not to say "hater of philosophy"! When did you discern that I cling to Chrysippus and the new Academy? Not before we, having a dwelling not of wood, but adorned with silver and gold, began to think about the garment of Christ and the rag, and, having labored much over them, moved from thought to action and now dwell in the Lord's abode? No, we are not attached to Chrysippus! Are you surprised that the bile boils within me and anger churns? Do you think I am unlike others, that there are no innards in my body where the angry spirit is born, and that I can therefore endure such an insult? No, your sacred soul! If you had beaten me, slapped my cheeks, pulled out all my hair, I would have endured it bravely, but now, when I do everything for Christ, and you, friend and judge, attribute to me friendship with Chrysippus and think of me as an apostate, having taken the side of Plato and the Academy, I do not know how to live on! Why do you impose the non-existent on even the mentioned lines, you who look down on everything? For the first one who spoke of them also introduced lines that "lie nowhere," acting very wisely and loftily. "To lie nowhere" does not mean "not to be." Lines do not "not exist," but when their length is conceived by the mind, then, as that scholar said, they "lie nowhere." The things related to these "non-existent lines" and the syllogisms you despise, I have connected with thoughts on more important subjects. These "non-existent" lines, let it be known to you, hater of words, lie at the foundation of all physical theory. The physical theory and our common Maximus, rather mine, for he is a philosopher, considers it the second virtue after practice, without claiming mathematical essence. And he who does not recognize the foundations of subjects takes away from syllogisms the conclusion, and in physical reasoning violates the integrity. When these two things are absent, the universal is neither a whole nor a goal for us, already nowhere marching, and not an accomplishment.

You see that this is already too much, that not looking [around oneself], not resorting to conclusions, and without thinking, without skillful dexterity [to climb] the cliffs of assumptions is irrationality and ignorance of ourselves.

If you will listen to me in anything, I will tell you this about yourself: do not think proudly about moving a mountain, and do not boast that you find no pleasure in reasoning. But find a plain and a deep hollow or a gaping chasm in the earth, descend there, hide at the bottom, lean over our and over pagan books, practice first in syllogisms and thus ascend to non-syllogistic knowledge...

This work was produced in association with:

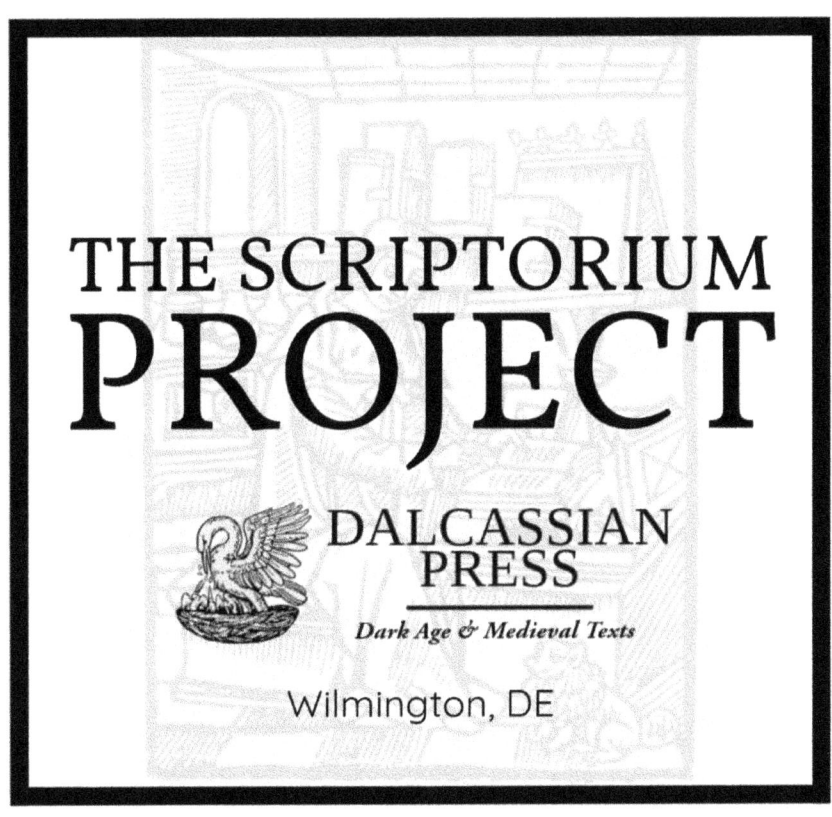

www.ingramcontent.com/pod-product-compliance
Lightning Source LLC
LaVergne TN
LVHW061050070526
838201LV00074B/5243